The Truth About Parenting

A Twin Mom's Handbook for the First 3 Years

ELIZABETH DE LUNA

The Truth About Parenting

A Twin Mom's Handbook for the First 3 Years

©2024, Elizabeth De Luna

Mission Statement: To tell the truth about parenting and be a guide
for others through their uncertainty.

ISBN: 979-8-35094-081-7
ISBN eBook: 979-8-35094-082-4

To my amazing husband and children who have taught me how to be the best mother I can be. I love you all tremendously.

Table of Contents

Introduction

When I first resigned from my job to become a full-time mom, I wanted to try to pursue something meaningful and artistic on the side. I was, and still am passionate about being the best mother I can be. Many people complimented me on habits I instilled in my children and would sporadically ask for my advice. I decided to write a book that could be helpful to new parents, especially new twin parents. I truly believe that this book can act as a small guide for parents who are unsure of what to do throughout their child's first three years of life. I held nothing back throughout the writing of this book. Although I am quite negative (though truthful) at times, every chapter ends with a message of positivity and hope.

1: The Truth about Parenting

How We Got Here

When I was in my early twenties, I did not want children. I truly never took the thought of it seriously. I like kids, and I can interact with them nicely for a couple of hours, but that is completely different from being in charge of them full time for eighteen plus years. My husband on the other hand was always adamant that he wanted kids, and he eventually talked me into it. My husband is a gem; he is loving, caring, patient, kind, brutally honest, and always giving in to doing things that I want to do. I definitely wanted to make him happy, and if having children was going to do that, I was all for it.

Right before I got pregnant with our twins, I was the one crying because we didn't have children yet. We were pretty good with our nephews, and we just wanted our own. I had no idea what I was in for. I'm sure a lot of people think, "I'm really good with kids, I'll be a great parent," but that is definitely not the case. Your own children will make you doubt yourself, your morals, your patience, and your anger. The thing is, you can't just test out having kids. You can't borrow a baby for three months, decide it's not for you, and then give them back. You're either all in or all out.

Before I had children, I used to see kids acting up in public places and I would think they were just spoiled. I would tell my husband, "Our kids are not going to behave like that; we will discipline them better." Now, I totally get it. All children are a handful and all children are different. There can be beautiful days without them having a breakdown, and other days when they may have back-to-back tantrums that you can't get away from. You can be a strict parent or a lenient parent, and it's still going to happen. You simply have to try to be understanding with them, but also teach them the correct way to handle situations.

Let's be clear, I absolutely love my children more than anyone and anything in the whole world. Everything I do is for them. I have a completely changed mindset, mentality, education plan, and career plan because of them. They bring me joy that I never thought I could feel in this life, but they also bring me the most frustration I've ever felt. I start this book with clarity on how parenting really is because I wish someone had told me. I hope the rest of this book offers helpful advice and tips for your child's first three years of life.

Why I'm Writing

A couple of days before my twins' second birthday, I jokingly told my husband I was going to write a book about how difficult it is to raise children. My husband and I feel like we were completely misled. Almost every married couple that we have ever known has had children. Most people make it seem like it's this big goal that they need to achieve in order to attain happiness. Once people have children, they may seem slightly frustrated, but overall happy.

Our siblings made it seem like it was nice having children. Being in a typical Hispanic family, we were always asked, "When are you all going to get pregnant?" Some of our friends would briefly explain to us the difficulty of parenting, but when they kept having children, we didn't think it could be too bad.

Now that we're going through it, my husband and I try our best to make it clear to other couples that having children is NOT a walk in the park, and it's definitely not the path that all couples need to take. Before we had our kids, we were very adventurous. We would skydive, bungee jump, travel when we were able to, go to any concert we wanted to, etc. We were having fun, and we thought we would be able to continue to do so. Now, we're counting down the days until we feel comfortable taking our children on a plane; we miss the adventure.

I truly didn't know how imprisoned I would feel as a mom. Now, I tell any young person I see that they don't have to have kids. When I'm in line at the grocery store and there's a teenager asking me, "Aw, are they twins? They're so cute," I smile and tell them, "Yes, but having kids is hard. Don't have kids if you don't want to, or at least wait until you're in your thirties." My husband always looks at me in disbelief, but it's just the truth! I really wish someone would have looked at me in desperation and said, "Do you like the freedom you have right now? Do you want that freedom forever? Then, don't have kids."

I'm sorry if this is a little negative. I really try to be a positive person, but if you're a new parent feeling like this, I want you to know that it's okay to have those feelings. I want to be transparent and tell it how it is in case anyone else can relate. Parenting is difficult, and it will always be the most difficult thing I will ever have to do. Parenting is stressful whether you have a newborn, 3-year-old, 15-year-old, or 30-year-old. You are constantly worried about your child's health and safety, it never goes away. However, parenthood gives you a grand purpose in life, and it can bring the most happiness and love that you will ever feel. Parenthood is similar to marriage; it's beautiful and fulfilling, but at the same time it's difficult and will require slight stress and work for the rest of your life.

Why It's Difficult

I might make it seem like it's absolutely terrifying to have children because in all honesty, when you're in the midst of a toddler tantrum or low on sleep, it does seem like the worst thing in the world is happening to you. One time I told my husband, "Why is parenting so hard? I'm so tired and I don't see it getting any easier." To which he replied, "Parenting is hard when you want what's best for your children. Parenting is easy for a lot of people because they don't always stress about what the best thing for their children is, but because you do stress about those things, it's difficult." I totally agree. Parenting is a challenge when you are intentional with the morals and values you want to instill in your children, and when you teach those values to them all day, every day. In a way, it's a good thing. If we thought parenting was easy, we would probably be parents who didn't care, or who are not very mindful with how they are raising their children.

Many parents are mindful of how and what they teach their children because they instinctively know they will not always be around. These parents want to pass down as much knowledge as they can from themselves to their children so their children can be prepared for any life situation. Raising children should not be an easy task. As Maria Montessori said, "We are to establish true and living methods for the training of future generations." We cannot slack off on parenting simply because we are tired, or do not feel that we have the capacity to better our children. We must do it for them, for their children, and for all of the generations to come. We must continuously evolve. I'm slightly familiar with Simon Sinek's work, and he calls this, "The Infinite Game." I've heard him discuss on podcasts that it is not about doing what is easy now, it's about doing what is ethical. Even if something is more difficult at the moment, if it is the right thing to do, it will pay off in the future.

If you have the intention of being a good parent, your stress levels increase even when your child is still in the womb. Once you find out the gender, you might think of gender-specific stresses that your child might go through. Once they're born, you are constantly worried about their health and safety. After some time, you feel so overwhelmed and you realize you haven't been correctly taking care of yourself or your spouse.

In all truthfulness, when my twins were about 4 months old, I had a split-second thought of leaving them and never looking back. The burden was just too much, and it would be so simple to be free again with no attachments, no worries. I never had that thought again, but I still occasionally cry over my lack of freedom as a mom. Some people might call this immature or selfish, but I believe it's normal. I wasn't extremely young when I became a mom, I was 25, but I never imagined how stressful and freedom-sucking parenting would feel. Who doesn't want their freedom? However, when you weigh the options of leaving and not leaving your children, staying with them has many more advantages and you will never regret it. They will bring you the most joy that you will ever feel.

Now I find that I cannot live without my children. Yes, I have my own life and I know how to live when they are not around, but I want them in my life. I choose them. I am being honest in this chapter because I don't think people are honest enough about the difficulties of parenting. Going forward, I want to share my journey with you and some tips to guide you through parenting. If you're reading this, you are probably a first-time parent, or twin parent, and might be feeling overwhelmed. The following chapters provide tips that I hope will guide you to be the best parent you can be.

While the second edit of this book was being done, I found out I was pregnant with our third child. My husband and I weren't trying, but we had just said, "If it happens, then it's meant to be." We are so excited to bring another baby into the world, and it has given me a clearer view of what I would like to include in this book. I will honestly take my own advice as I go through another baby phase as an experienced mom.

2: The Journey Begins

Doctors

I try to be as natural as possible in most aspects of my life. Therefore, when we were beginning to discuss getting pregnant, I asked all the new moms I knew about their OB, and if they had a vaginal delivery. I had heard about the high C-Section rates, and I didn't want to be a part of those statistics. I chose a doctor who many of my friends and acquaintances had their babies vaginally with, and I felt confident with my decision. Once I found out I was having twins, I often stressed to the doctor that I wanted to have them vaginally. He would tell me it was not common with twins, but we would see what would happen.

Even though C-sections can be lifesaving, they are often not necessary. In 2018, about 21.1% percent of global pregnancies were delivered by C-Section. This is almost double the amount of C-section rates from the year 2000. In more affluent neighborhoods, C-Section rates are 5 times more likely to happen than in impoverished regions due to the use of hospitals and private facilities. My advice is to do your research even before you get pregnant, or soon after you find out, to see which options are right for you. Everyone has different preferences, but you do not want to have any regrets in the future.

After my preeclampsia formed in my seventh month of pregnancy, my doctor said the delivery would have to be a C-Section as the risk was too high. I was shocked to hear this because I still felt healthy and I was not on any medication for preeclampsia. Aside from that, both of my babies were head down in my womb. The day before my C-Section was scheduled, I was still asking how I could have the babies vaginally, to which they told me I would have to get flown by helicopter to a children's specialty hospital if I wanted to even try to deliver them vaginally. I truly considered this, but it was an extreme step forward, so my husband and I decided not to. I had even discussed delivering them at home, but it's not the norm anymore and everyone was worried for my health and the health of the babies.

The day before I was scheduled to go in for my C-Section, I did squats to see if the babies would come on their own. I think the squats worked, as my water broke a couple of hours later. Once we got to the hospital, I was only one centimeter dilated and the C-Section still went on.

I know I tried my best during my pregnancy to deliver my babies vaginally, but if I could go back, I would consider getting a midwife to assist with it all. Whatever your choice is, make sure you are comfortable with it. If you are not comfortable with your doctor, hospital, or birthing plan, make sure you change them. At the time, I was comfortable with my decisions, and now I look back and have some regrets, but we just have to move forward from our regrets. At the end of the day, I'm happy my babies and I are safe and healthy.

If there is a birthing center near you, I would consider them first. Midwives are much more knowledgeable on the natural practices of pregnancy than OBGYN's. As far as I know, medical students are not being taught how to perform twin or breech vaginal deliveries anymore, which is causing C-Section rates to soar. If you are comfortable delivering with a midwife, then I would seriously consider it.

With my new-found pregnancy, I am adamant on having a vaginal delivery. One of the hospitals in my town does not allow Vaginal Birth After Cesarean (VBAC's), so I looked into all the OBs from the hospital that does allow VBACs. I called eleven different doctor's offices to ask if their doctor performs VBAC's. To my surprise, most of them said no and I was left with two choices (who have many patients and a very long wait time). Therefore, I have chosen to deliver in a city about three hours away just so I can have a natural home birth at my aunt's house. I honestly don't even want to step foot in a hospital if I don't have to. Birthing is natural and I want to experience it that way.

Pregnancy

Trying to get pregnant is a blast, you get to have lots of sex! Some women feel the sexiest they've ever felt when they are pregnant, and some feel like Shamu. I was somewhere in between. I was extremely bloated with morning sickness the first couple of months. Around months three and four, I was awkwardly showing (people could have assumed I was just gaining weight). Months five and six were the months I felt really cute. I loved my perfectly round belly and being able to feel the babies moving around. During month seven (pretty much my last month of being pregnant), I gained about forty pounds. My legs were swollen beyond belief due to preeclampsia, and I was constantly going to doctors' appointments while trying to prolong my delivery. I was huge and uncomfortable, and I couldn't wait to get the babies out.

Preeclampsia is fairly common in pregnancies, but I never thought I would develop it. Preeclampsia is basically high blood pressure when you are pregnant. It can be detrimental for the baby (or babies) and mother. I initially thought preeclampsia, along with gestational diabetes, only developed from an unhealthy diet.

From day one of my pregnancy, I either walked or did yoga every single day. I was vegetarian at the time and hardly ever ate fast food or unhealthy foods. Up until month six, I was on track with the pregnancy weight gain charts, and thought I was doing great health-wise.

Month seven came around and I was told I had preeclampsia. That's when I ended up gaining forty pounds. I desperately wanted my twins to go through the birth canal, but with my conditions, it was nearly impossible (according to the doctors). I went from weighing 116 pounds to 170 pounds; I was ashamed to even look at my last weigh in at the hospital, but what could I do? Towards the end of my pregnancy, I would explain to my husband how uncomfortable I felt. I told him it was difficult to be comfortable because my body was not my own; I was sharing it with two small humans and I had little control of how I felt physically.

If you are uncomfortable being pregnant, don't sweat it. The good thing is, it lasts less than a year, and it will be over soon. The best thing you can do is be active, eat healthy, and stay positive. Besides that, whatever happens is out of your control. Don't obsess with your weight loss or weight gain, just do your best. I know pregnancy can be uncomfortable, but it is definitely worth it.

NICU Babies

I delivered our beautiful baby boys at thirty-four weeks. They were both in the four-pound range and had to stay in the NICU for eighteen days. I knew NICU visits were common with twins, but I never thought our babies would end up there; it's just something you don't want to worry yourself about if you don't have to. However, our babies did end up there, and for over two weeks. I was blindsided by this. I never would have imagined the emotional effects having our babies in the NICU would have on me.

Having your newborn baby (or babies) taken away from you instantly after delivery and not being able to be with them full-time within days after birth is incredibly unnatural and can be psychologically taxing on parents. I was truly depressed. Now, I look back on it as a "maybe it was meant to be" situation because I was able to ease into nightly feedings (through pumping at my own pace), and we were able to move in and set up our new house before bringing the babies home. I was never diagnosed with postpartum depression, but I know I was depressed; there's no other feeling like it. You feel lifeless, like a zombie that other people are always trying to bring back to life. Thankfully, when we brought our boys home I was able to snap out of depression, and went straight into exhaustion.

If you know someone who has their babies in the NICU, or if you have your baby in the NICU, please know that you are not alone. It is normal to feel sadness. According to the National Library of Medicine, "Mothers of children in the NICU show higher levels of depression and anxiety symptoms than those with healthy term children." It may seem like a lifetime when your baby is in the NICU, but the time will pass. Stay positive and think about all of the wonderful times you and your child have ahead of you. Also, be sure that no one stops you from holding or breastfeeding your baby. They may live at the hospital for a short while, but they are yours.

If you are a parent of multiples, be prepared to have them in the NICU. Know that it is difficult, but it is do-able. You've got this. It is not your fault if you are depressed; you will be able to overcome this because your babies will make you stronger. They are worth being happy for.

A natural birthing podcast I recommend:

- Problems with our Medical Birthing System with Dr. Stuart Fischbein - The Ellen Fisher Podcast

A natural birthing documentary I recommend:

- The Business of Being Born

3: The Essentials

Breastfeeding

Breastfeeding is hard, but breastfeeding is also really easy. I was adamant on breastfeeding because it is the purest and most natural form of nutrition you can give your baby. When you are a first-time mom though, it can be intimidating. Other moms are always talking about breastfeeding being painful, or the baby not being able to latch so they had to switch to formula. Our society also doesn't help by making baby formula so common and readily available. Almost half of U.S. moms decide to have their baby on formula. Most OB's or pediatricians do not push mothers to breastfeed, and at many hospitals you have to ask for advice on how to do it rather than someone educating or encouraging you to do it.

However, breastfeeding is extremely beneficial for your child. Breastfed babies have lower risks of multiple diseases and infections; they will have these benefits throughout their lifetime. Breastfeeding is also beneficial for the mom as it can protect her from diseases such as cancer, it burns calories so you can take the baby weight off faster, and one of my favorite things about breastfeeding is that it's free! Most families spend over $1,000 on formula for 1 year, but why do that when you can breastfeed? If you exclusively breastfeed, you also don't have to worry about buying and washing bottles.

If you're staying home with the baby, you really don't have to worry about pumping. It is much simpler to latch your baby and then you won't have to take the time to pump or clean bottles afterwards. I know it may be difficult to breastfeed for working moms, but yours and your baby's health comes first. Your job should make accommodations for you to pump or breastfeed your child every two-to-three hours at work; it can be done. Most states have laws implemented that say employers must support breastfeeding and pumping moms.

After delivering my babies, I was not able to see them at all hours of the day because they were in the NICU. Therefore, my only choice was to pump. The first six times I pumped, my breasts did not produce anything. I felt very discouraged, exhausted, and in pain. I honestly don't know if I would have continued pumping if it wasn't for my husband. He encouraged me to not give up, and when I produced my first drops of milk from each breast, we were both so excited.

If you feel like you can't do it, please don't give up. Find yourself a cheerleader or guide that will help you through it. Someone who has experience with breastfeeding would be best, but anyone can help to keep you motivated. Remember that breastfeeding is natural. Many moms believe they cannot produce milk, but most moms can, it is only human nature. We are mammals and we are meant to feed our babies. I know there are certain circumstances that may not allow you to give your child 100% breastmilk, but give them as much as you can, if you can. You can ask your hospital to speak with a lactation consultant, and you can even find more lactation consultants online. In Texas, there's a free lactation hotline you can call. Here's the number: 855-550-6667.

If you are looking for a breast pump, there are always free options available. If you have health insurance, call them and ask them how you can choose your free pump. If you do not have insurance, programs like WIC should allow you to choose a free pump. When I would pump, I would often look at YouTube videos to see how I could produce more milk. Some videos were helpful, but others were overwhelming. If you see videos of moms producing large amounts of milk, please don't be intimidated. Remember that babies need a very small amount of milk in the beginning, and then you will gradually produce more as they need more. No matter how much your body is producing, be grateful that it is making nutritious milk for your baby.

Formula

Personally, my twins received half breastmilk and half formula. From the beginning, the doctors stated that they needed more milk to grow, and gave them formula in the NICU. We agreed to that because we were truly worried about their health, growth, and development. We are so happy they did have breast milk though because of all the benefits it will give them throughout their lives.

If you are giving your child formula, whether part-time or full-time, be sure that it is the formula you believe is best for them. There are an overwhelming amount of options out there, so it is good to do your research before you decide. At the hospital, the nurses were giving our twins regular cow's milk formula. My husband and I were uneasy with this as we know dairy is not optimal for the human body. The nurses and doctors insisted that they needed cow's milk to grow and advised against us giving them soy or plant-based formula.

Right before our twins turned 2 months, one of our friends was over at our house and she was explaining a time when a doctor wanted to put her daughter on medication, and she flat out told the doctor no. She was not comfortable with the side effects of the medication and was going to treat her daughter in a more natural way. She said, "She's my daughter and I will make the decisions I believe are best for her." From that moment on, I took that advice and ran with it. So, since our twins have been 2 months old, they have not ingested any dairy products, and we are very satisfied with that. Their pediatrician said they would not grow on a fully vegan diet, but they are usually around the 50th percentile at all of their appointments. They are beautiful, healthy vegan children. I know doctors and nurses can be intimidating, but they are still part of a large healthcare system that does not always recommend what is best for the patient. If your child is drinking formula, do your research and choose the one that you believe is best for your baby.

Cloth Diapers

Right before I got pregnant, I went down many rabbit holes on YouTube about environmentalism and things we can do to help the Earth. One tip that always came up was cloth diapers, but I never thought much of it because I didn't have a baby. A couple of months into my pregnancy, my husband kept going on and on about getting an electric car and how it would be good for the Earth if we didn't drive a gas vehicle. At this point, I was seriously preparing for our twins and the thought of having disposable diapers on them just didn't sit well with me. Disposables are bad for the Earth, have unknown chemicals in them, and are very costly. We also had double the expenses coming at us with our twins and we wanted to minimize the things we needed in order to save money. Therefore, I told him we could definitely get an electric car, but only if we used cloth diapers with our babies.

Cloth diapering has been a relatively simple process; much simpler than what people might believe. We decided to use pocket diapers because we felt that was the easiest for us, but there are other options out there. Pocket diapers come in two parts: a waterproof outline, and an absorbent insert. We believed these cloth diapers would be the most absorbent because we could add additional liners inside if we needed to. We waited about two months to use them because most of these diapers are for babies 8 or more pounds, and our babies were born at 4 pounds each. Once we started using cloth diapers, we returned all of the disposable diapers we had been gifted, and our boys never wore disposable diapers again. We even took our cloth diapers on a three-day out-of-town trip and it was very easy. We just stuffed the dirty diapers in a wet bag, and washed them as soon as we got home!

Overall, cloth diapering could not have been easier. We loved that we never had to spend money on diapers at the store, and most of our cloth diapers were paid for through our baby registry. We are very grateful for our washer and dryer as they do most of the work, and we just have to prep the diapers once they're out of the dryer. Some poops were extremely messy and it was difficult to clean the diapers when only one of us was home, but we always got it done. We have no regrets on cloth diapering and we wish more people did it. When our boys started to have explosive diapers, we questioned if they were worth it. However, when we would hear about our friends' babies also having leaky diapers in disposables, we realized it can happen with any type of diaper you decide to use.

Cloth diapers can save an abundance of garbage that ends up in landfills. They also save families over $1,500 per child. If you have 3 kids, that's $4,500! Cloth diapers can be used for all of your children and they can even be sold, so you make a profit once you're done with them! We've sold half of ours so far and made $100. You could never make money back by using disposable diapers.

When it comes to wipes, we tried to use reusable wipes, but were a little intimidated, so we bought disposable wipes in bulk. One of our good friends told us recently that she was also intimidated by the soap solution most people use with reusable wipes, so she just used a wet towelette and it worked fine for her family. Therefore, she saved even more money by not buying disposable wipes, and she is reusing all of her diapering materials for her second child. Now that I'm expecting my third child, I'm so happy

I don't have to worry about buying diapers. All of ours are in good condition and can be used again!

I should add here that we personally wash our cloth diapers every three days. We run a tight ship, so it always gets done. Some people don't like cloth diapering because, 1. They are expensive up front, and 2. It gives you more laundry to do. I counteract those individuals with, 1. You can ask for them through your gift registry, purchase them with baby shower money, or buy used ones for a discounted price online or from a friend, and 2. The washer and dryer do the work for you! If you're wondering how many cloth diapers you will need, we had about 20 per child and we did just fine with that. If you want to wash less often, then you would need more diapers.

I love the Nora's Nursery cloth diapers sold on Amazon. Most pocket diapers come with only 1 liner inside, but we would put 2 liners to make them more absorbent. We put 3 liners in the night-time diapers so they can last all night. For liners, we like the Naturally Nature bamboo liners sold on Amazon to add to our Nora's Nursery diapers.

We have a special hamper with a wet bag that we use for dirty diapers. When we had to clean poop, we would just go outside and wash the diaper off in our backyard. We tried to clean them indoors, but it didn't really work for us. When it came to washing, we would wash in a specific way to clean the diapers correctly and gently, as follows:

1. Set a rinse cycle with detergent only - no fabric softener. Do this with cold water.

2. Set a regular wash cycle with detergent and bleach (we like the seventh generation bleach) - no fabric softener. Do this with hot water.

3. Dry the diapers on the lowest heat setting for about 1.5 hours.

A good friend of mine, Raquel, assisted me in editing this book. She is a fellow cloth diapering parent, and recommends the Cloth Diaper Wash and Care group on Facebook. They can help you tailor your laundry routine and help with any cloth diapering questions you may have.

Washing and drying the diapers would usually take us 4 - 5 hours overall, and about 20 minutes to fill them (if you use pocket diapers). I know that sounds like a lot of time, but remember, the washer and dryer do the work for you! You can go about your day as the diapers are washing and drying. My husband and I personally liked to fill the diapers as we got a short break from the boys and would just put on a podcast or music to listen to while filling them.

If you decide to use cloth diapers, be sure that all caretakers of the child are willing to do it as well. I am lucky my mom was more than happy to help us with them when she would take care of our boys, but some caretakers or daycares may not allow it.

YouTube videos I recommend for cloth diapering:

- "Everything I Wish I knew Before Cloth Diapering" - LoeppkysLife

- "What I've Learned from One Year of Cloth Diapering" - LoeppkysLife

4: How to Cure an Exhausted Parent

Sleep Training

By the second day our boys were home with us, we were exhausted. Everyone knows babies are not the best at sleeping through the night, but does anyone ever talk about how difficult having a crying baby all night in your bedroom is? If you've never experienced hearing a crying baby in the middle of the night, it will be a complete shocker to you once you become a parent. When I would ask my husband why no one warned us about the exhaustion parenting brought, he would say, "It's easy for people to forget how hard it is."

By the time the boys turned four months, I could not take it anymore. We had given up on warming bottles and pumping during the night, so I was just latching them. They were EACH waking up about every two hours and they would do this one hour apart, so I was up every hour. I was crazy sleep deprived. I was weary of allowing them to sleep in the bed with us for fear of rolling over them, and the fear of sleeping with them until they're ten years old, so they were likely waking up to be held and comforted as well.

I did some research and figured out how to sleep train our boys. I highly suggest sleep training to anyone who believes they can keep a schedule. If you sleep train, your children can get used to putting themselves to sleep and sleeping on their own all night. During the first week of sleep training, our family was uneasy about us letting them cry it out. By the second week, everyone was amazed that we could just take the boys into their rooms (they each had their own room by this point), lay them down while they were still awake, say, "I love you, goodnight," and then they would fall asleep on their own within ten minutes.

Ever since we sleep trained them at their 4-month mark, our twins have been sleeping through the night from 7PM - 7AM. We love this, as we can relax and not worry about having to wake up for them during the night. We can also go on an occasional date at 8PM if we have a sitter, and the sitter just has to sit down, watch TV, and make sure the boys are still asleep through the monitor. Certain nights are the exception when they will wake up for some reason, but it honestly doesn't happen more than 5 times a year.

The Importance of Schedules

Sleep training works for most families that can keep a schedule. If you are able to keep them, schedules allow your child to be ready for transitions, and can help decrease tantrums. Some people have asked us if our boys give us trouble when it's bath or nap time, and the answer is always no. I can't imagine how difficult it is to have to coerce a child into these tasks every day just because they are not used to completing them at a scheduled time.

You don't need to be rigid about your schedule (I was at the beginning, because I wanted to be sure we kept it), but it is good to keep within a certain time range for each activity every day. For example, right now our boys know that this is their schedule as 2-year-olds:

7:00 AM	Wake up & brush teeth.
7:30 AM	Have breakfast.
8:00 AM	Play on their own while we clean up the kitchen.
8:30 AM	Read books and sing learning songs.
9:00 AM	Go to the park and the grocery store if we need any items.
11:00 AM	Lunch.
11:30 AM	Free play time with their toys.
1:00 PM	Nap time.
3:00 PM	More play time.
4:00 PM	Art/School time.
4:45 PM	Dinner time.
5:30 PM	Play time/ Read books.
6:00 PM	Evening walk.
6:50 PM	Bath time routine.
7:20 PM	Bedtime.

Our schedule is like this every single day and we really believe this is why there are no tantrums or breakdowns when we are transitioning to something new. Sometimes we will get pushback on which park they want to go to or what they would like to eat, and when that happens, we try to give them two different options on what they would like. Tantrums are still going to happen with a schedule, but schedules are great for decreasing them and easing into a proper sleep schedule. When the seasons change, our schedules change as well, but wake and sleep times are always consistent.

Sleep Training Details

You can begin sleep training when your baby is 3 or 4 months old, and they will most likely be sleeping 11 - 12 hours through the night by the time they are 5 months. We were in heaven after sleep training and looked forward to our evenings together. Other parents would talk about their 1-year-olds waking up at night and how they were exhausted, and we were so grateful we weren't going through that. Honestly, we were still tired, but not nearly as tired as we were the first 4 months with 2 newborns.

When sleep training, it's important to remember that most babies need three naps plus their additional 12-hour sleep at night. As they get older, they will drop down to two naps (around 8 months), and then down to one nap (between 12 - 18 months). Keeping a sleep training schedule, or just a schedule in general is more difficult when traveling, but it can be done. When we travel, we give ourselves about an hour of leeway compared to our normal schedule. For example, we might eat brunch at 10 AM, or lunch at 12 PM when traveling instead of our 11 AM norm. We also might not nap until 2 PM and then sleep until 8:30 PM, but we try to keep the schedule as similar as possible so we can ease right back into our routine when we return home.

If you're wondering what your baby's sleep schedule should look like, they have many online. If you have a 5-month-old, just search, "Sleep schedule for a 5-month-old", and examples will come out. I always clicked on images and chose one I liked; I believe I always liked the Huckleberry website. Our boys took two full naps, and a 30-minute power nap until they were about 9 months old. After this, it was two, 2-hour naps (which I loved because I would clean and do things during the first nap, and then nap myself during the second nap). When the boys were about 18 months, they dropped their morning nap and only had an afternoon nap, which we are still so grateful for.

When you put your baby down for a nap or for bedtime, you should have a small sleep routine in order to ease them into sleep training. Two things that helped us before we fully sleep trained were a white noise machine and a sleep sack. Once our babies heard the white noise and we put the sleep sacks on them, they knew it was time to go to sleep. We used sleep sacks until they were about 12 months old and we plan on using the white noise machine for a long time.

How We Sleep Trained

Here are some steps you can follow if you are planning on sleep training, but I would also recommend reading specific sleep training books and watching sleep training YouTube videos.

1. Be sure your child is accommodated in their long-term room. This can be a room shared with a sibling as well, but for us, separate rooms worked best.

2. Set up a monitor and camera so you can ensure their safety when you are not in the room.

3. Be sure they will be in the same crib, or bed, for the next 3 months so you are not constantly changing things on them.

4. Buy a white noise machine so it can help drown out noise from the rest of the house. Be sure the white noise is not louder than 50 decibels; there are free apps to measure

decibels. Our boys sleep with their white noise all night and during their naps.

5. Buy blackout curtains so the room is dark and they are able to sleep better. For the first two years, we simply put a blanket over the window because we hadn't bought curtains. Do what works best for you.

6. Make sure their room is a calm environment. You do not want any electronics or large, distracting toys that will affect their sleep. Make sure your baby is not too overstimulated about 30 minutes before they go down for a nap or before they go to bed for the night. Turn off the TV, dim the lights, and read some books quietly so they can wind down before they sleep.

7. Ease into a set schedule. After the third day of that schedule, you can begin sleep training.

8. Officially beginning sleep training: Day 1 of sleep training will be the hardest. You will start during their first nap. Make sure your baby has been fed and burped correctly. Make sure they have a dry diaper and are comfortable. Then, you will go to their room and tell them that you love them and it is time for them to go to sleep. You will then put your baby down in their crib while they are awake. They will likely cry and scream if they are used to being rocked to sleep, but they should fall asleep within 15 minutes. If they don't fall asleep after 15 minutes, go into their room and rub their belly, but do not pick them up. Tell them you love them and they need to go to sleep, then leave their room and wait another 15 minutes. Do this cycle until they fall asleep. Repeat this cycle with their other naps, and with their nighttime sleep.

9. Nighttime Feedings: When your baby wakes up for their first nighttime feeding, put a 15-minute timer on your phone and wait. They may go back to sleep before the time is done, but if they are still crying after 15 minutes, you can go in their room, rub their belly (don't pick them up), tell them you love them, that they are safe, and that it is time to go to sleep. Then, you will leave their room and put another 15-minute timer. If they are still crying after this timer, you can go in and feed them. Once you are done feeding and burping them correctly, you will place them down awake. Because you are getting them used to being uninterrupted at night, you do not need to change their diaper if it is dry. Repeat this every time they wake up crying for the next week. By the end of the week, they should definitely have dropped a nighttime feeding, and will hopefully be sleeping through the night. Our first twin slept his first full night after the 3rd day of sleep training, and our second twin slept his first full night after the 5th day. Every baby is different. Be patient and don't give up. It will be worth it!

Sleep training is not only helpful for parents, but it also allows the child to grow and develop at a healthy rate. Don't be discouraged if your baby cries for the full 15 minutes when you put them down, they just need to get used to putting themselves to sleep. Try to distract yourself from their crying by taking a shower, washing the dishes, or vacuuming. The crying will definitely stop after one week. You can put pictures on their wall, or a mobile and encourage them to look at that while they are falling asleep. As long as you know they are safe, there is no reason to feel guilty about their crying.

Sleep training books I recommend:

- On Becoming Babywise - Robert Bucknam and Gary Ezzo
- The Baby Sleep Solution - Suzy Giordano

YouTube Video I recommend for sleep training:

- "Sleep Routine with Twin Babies" - Kendry Atkins

5: Baby Minimalism

Naturally, I am a minimalist. My mom always taught my sister and I to get rid of things we hadn't used in about a year. Growing up, our house was always very clean and everything was in its place. Once I got married, our 600-square-foot apartment was just as tidy; we only had what we needed and nothing more. When I got pregnant, I knew babies needed a lot of things, but I was sure I would keep it as minimal as possible. When I found out we were having twins, it was an even harder challenge, but I knew I could do it.

I highly encourage couples to get as little as possible when expecting. Babies grow out of everything they will need by the time they are 3 years old. It's ridiculous how much we buy for them and how little of it we end up using. When it comes to essential/large items for a newborn, all you need is a car seat, clothes, diapers, a crib, and possibly a baby wrap to carry them around; that's it! If you are breastfeeding, you don't even need any bottles or formula. If you're bottle feeding, you honestly only need about eight bottles. We only had eight bottles with our twins and it worked out.

I learned from my best friend that you don't even need a baby carrier car seat. I always find these carriers to be so bulky and uncomfortable. For our boys, we bought a 3-in-1 car seat and they're still using it now that they are 3 years old. When we had to get them down somewhere, we just had them in our Baby K'tan (a wearable carrier), or held them. Family always wanted to hold them as well, so it worked out. Once they turned 5 months and were more stable, we would put them in a double stroller which we used until they were 2. This double stroller was a hand me down we exchanged for a $40 gift card. After they turned 2, we just had them walk everywhere with us. Now that they're almost 3, they can go on one-hour walks, or they use their scooters.

When it comes to bedding, most couples switch from a bassinet to a crib at about 3 months. If a crib fits in your bedroom, you honestly don't need a bassinet at all. A crib will serve the same purpose as a bassinet does. We had bassinets for the twins, but now that we are expecting our third baby, I plan on only using a crib for the first 12 months. Because we had twins, we purchased mini cribs that both fit in our room. Once your child begins to stand, around 9 months, cribs can get scary as babies will eventually attempt to climb out of them.

Our boys used their mini cribs for about 10 months (from the time they were 4 months - 14 months). At 14 months, we decided to go the Montessori route and got them floor beds. We loved this because we weren't afraid of them falling out of a crib or off of a bed. If they did fall, it was a very small drop from their crib mattress to the floor. I plan on having our next child use a floor bed when they are about 12 months old. We recently got rid of the floor bed frames so our boys could have a larger mattress, so now they just have a full-size mattress on the floor. They don't need any fancy furniture in the way when they're playing in their rooms. They love that they can just bounce and play on their beds without the risk of hitting anything hard. The only worry I had when switching them to a floor bed was them eventually being able to open their doors and leave the room. Their rooms are upstairs, so I definitely didn't want that. We decided to switch the locks on their doors so we could ensure their safety. We will likely switch the locks back when they understand how a toddler clock works, so they can leave their room freely.

When our boys were infants, we tried not to keep them in a playpen, and had them on the floor all the time. We honestly only used the playpen if they were napping at my parent's house. I considered buying one of those large floor play pens so they would be safe while playing, but we simply corralled them with our sofas for a few months. Once they were a little older (about 14 months), we decided that they could roam freely and just had a baby gate for the stairs. In order to do this, you need to make sure all of your lower cabinets are baby-safe, or simply explain to them which cabinets they can and cannot use. They will learn quickly.

We never invested in walkers and bouncers. These items were things that did not sit right with me; I wanted their legs to get strong naturally, with their own movements. Something that was helpful when the boys were about 3 - 11 months were little baby chairs. I would put them there when I had to wash dishes or go to the restroom. Those were worth the buy, and they were very affordable. The ones we had were simple with no vibrations or sounds. Preparing for our third baby, I will most likely just use a breastfeeding pillow as a chair for them. Another thing I wouldn't invest in, is a full-blown changing table. You will end up changing your baby everywhere but there. Beds are usually more comfortable, just don't leave your baby unattended. We also never bought a "diaper bag", we just bought a large adult backpack and still use that.

Once your baby begins to crawl and get around on their own, it is important to babyproof the house. They sell all-in-one kits for this that can be helpful. Remember to cover all electrical outlets, lock any cabinets that have harmful chemicals or materials, and place baby gates on the bottom and top of stairs. Once they are tall enough to reach locks and knobs on doors, be sure to babyproof the knob, or place a latch on the door so they cannot open it. Baby proof items are essential; you don't want any harm happening to your baby.

Overall, just tread lightly when it comes to baby lists that you see online. Yes, you will need many things they recommend, but you definitely won't need them all. If you feel like it's something that can wait, then hold off until you decide if you'll need it. When it comes to bottle and wipe warmers, I easily did without them, but everyone is different. To me, less is more, especially when you will only use these brand new items for two years. If you can buy second hand at thrift stores or online, that's even better. You could also ask for money at your baby shower instead of having a registry so you can buy exactly what you want.

Once your baby reaches a new developmental stage, you may want to take time to clean out what they don't need anymore. I would personally clean out every three months because they grow so quickly at the beginning of their life. You can set these items aside for your next child, or share them with someone who you know may need them. If there are large items you are looking to get rid of, you can always sell them and make some money. I stress minimalism on baby items for two reasons: to save money & to not overwhelm the parent and child.

When it comes to having your child become more independent around 18 months, I suggest getting a stool for the bathroom so they can practice brushing their teeth and hair independently. I also suggest a learning tower so they can help you with meals in the kitchen, but a stool can also work just fine for this. These aren't essential baby items, but essential toddler items.

Items that are essential:

- 3-in-1 Car seat

- Crib, Crib Mattress, & Crib Sheets

- Bottles & Formula (if not breastfeeding)

- Breast Pump & Freezer Bags (if you'll be away from the baby)

- Diapers (cloth or disposable), Wipes, & Diaper Cream
- Clothes
- Baby Swaddles & Sleep Sacks
- Baby Monitor
- White Noise Machine
- Wearable Baby Carrier Wrap
- Stroller
- High Chair (Preferably one that converts to a table chair)
- Bibs or burp cloths
- Backpack (You can use one that you already have!)
- Babyproof All-in-One Kit
- Baby Chair (or nursing pillow)
- Thermometer
- Baby Bathtub
- Washcloths for bathtime
- 1 Hamper for clothes and 1 hamper for cloth diapers
- Books
- Wooden toys
- Stool for bathroom
- Learning tower for kitchen

Items that are NOT essential:

- Bassinet

- Car Seat Carrier

- Bottle Warmers (If we did have to warm a bottle, we would place it in a bowl of hot water for 2 minutes, and it was good to go)

- Wipe Warmers

- Playpens

- Changing Tables or Pads

- Diaper Pail

- Walkers & Bouncers

6: Raising Baby Geniuses

Learning Toys

From the time your child is born to the time they are 6 years old, they are capable of learning more than what you could ever imagine. You often hear adults saying, "They are sponges right now." Maria Montessori called this, "The Absorbent Mind" because they soak up all of the information that surrounds them during this developmental period. With that being said, it is important for parents to be vigilant of the information their child is acquiring. It is a full-time job, but it is necessary to filter what kinds of books, toys, and shows your child is playing with or watching. You want to be sure these objects teach your child the truth about life and your morals as a family. Our morals as a family are to teach realistic and truthful education and how to be a peaceful, loving, and empathetic person.

When it comes to toys, we automatically asked our family not to get us any battery-operated toys. We didn't want our boys to be overstimulated. We mostly asked for wooden toys or books. When our boys were about 3 months old, I decided I wanted to take the Montessori approach, and my mother-in-law offered to get us the Lovevery subscription boxes. These boxes were very helpful while I was working. I didn't have time to see what toys were going to be educational for our boys at their rapidly developing stages, so I loved the automatic subscription. Now that I'm not working, the subscription still makes it so easy for me to rotate their learning toys and saves me time on researching what is best for them. If you feel like you do not have the capacity to do research on learning toys, I highly suggest Lovevery. You can use the toys for a long time and just have them in a toy rotation. I know the subscriptions can be expensive, but you can definitely ask for them as gifts. Now that we have our third baby on the way, I'm so happy I have these toys that are sorted for our baby's age-appropriate development.

We had a lot of hand-me-down clothes from my nephews, so when it came to Christmas and birthday gifts, we often asked our family not to get them clothes. For their 3rd birthday, we did an Amazon registry and we were really satisfied. They received some clothes, lots of books, and learning items we were in need of.

I know it can be awkward, but if you sit down with your family beforehand and explain the things your child needs to continue their education, they will understand. If they still get you items that you feel your child should not use, you can return the item, or only have your child use those toys when the relatives who gifted them are visiting. If you're not sure which learning toys to get, I highly recommend watching videos from The Hapa Family on YouTube. I also love Melissa and Doug toys; you can find them on Amazon, as well as Walmart and Target.

The Importance of Reading

I have a natural inclination towards books. I've loved them since I was a child, and I continued to love reading into my adulthood. I love reading so much that I became a librarian. You could say I'm biased towards the benefits of books, but in this day in age I just think reading is so much more beneficial than having a screen in front of you. Newborn babies don't need much entertainment, they are usually interested in what everyone in their surroundings are doing. I know it can seem like you must entertain your baby all day, every day, but you really don't need to.

Everything is new to a baby and they will simply enjoy being with you and watching what you are doing when you're folding laundry, washing dishes, cooking dinner, etc. I have vivid memories of having one of my boys in the Baby K'tan carrier whenever they were uneasy while I was washing dishes or vacuuming. They would simply watch me and what I was doing while I completed household chores. Sometimes they just wanted to be close to me and it really helped to calm their mood. During the times I wanted to enjoy my babies when they were awake (usually a little before or after feedings), I would read to them.

I started reading to our boys as soon as we brought them home. I had a basket of books in our living room and our bedroom, so the books were always readily available. Our babies were often intrigued by the pictures in the books, and I know the vocabulary they heard was beneficial to them as well. Sometimes I wouldn't get to finish the book as they were so young and just wanted my one-on-one attention, but for the most part, they would listen. Before they turned 6 months, I would give them little crinkly books that they could hold and play with or simply look at.

By the time our boys were sitting up on their own (around 6 months) we made sure we had a lot of board books on hand. I recommend having board books from the time your child is 6 months to about 2-and-a-half years old. At 6 months, babies are able to hold a book in their hands and look at pictures on their own. By 8 months they may be able to turn the pages on their own if they see you do it often enough. Babies are usually drawn to real life, non-fiction images, so that is what we would try to give them. Some babies might want to bite books, especially when teething. When this happens, you can tell them calmly that you do not want them to bite the book, and take it away from them for a short while.

When your child reaches the 2-year mark, they will begin to communicate more often, and you will become aware of all the things they have learned within the past 2 years. When our boys turned 2, I had an instinctual feeling that I wanted to teach them the alphabet. I mentioned this to my mom and she bought them some alphabet books. After a few weeks of reading these books, our boys learned their letters in no time. We paired the books with a wooden alphabet puzzle and they knew all their letter names and sounds right before they turned 2-and-a-half. They learned their colors before they were 2, and their numbers around their 2-year mark all because of the books we read to them. Some people were surprised, but we think it's just a common age they learn these things. We never forced them to read these books, but we made the books available. Plus, they loved it when we read to them.

At about the age of 1 (probably even before), we began reading two bedtime stories before bed and it is a habit I hope continues for the rest of their life. We have age-appropriate books for them all over the house, so they often ask us to read to them. When we put them down for a nap, they have books in their rooms they can browse through before falling asleep on their own, or after they wake up. My yearning to have no screen time resulted in the amount of books our boys are used to reading. This will hopefully be a lifelong habit for them. When they are bored or they need to kill some time, I hope they will pick up a book rather than opting for any sort of screen.

If you haven't started reading to your child, it's never too late to begin. Children are so flexible and they pick up habits quickly (good or bad). I know books can be expensive, but you can take advantage of library books, Little Free Library books, books purchased from garage sales, books from thrift stores, hand-me-downs, or ask for gifted books! If your children are interested in a specific topic, try to get books about that. For us, our boys are interested in colors, construction vehicles, trains, planes, and animals, so we try to stick to these topics.

Screen Time

When my best friend had her first child, she told me she was not going to allow him to have screen time. She explained how she simply felt it wasn't the best for him as it's not even good for adults to have too much screen time, so she wanted to steer clear from it for a while. A couple of months later, I was reading a required book for one of my college courses. The book stated how screens can be harmful to children, but how it is normal for screens to be shown to them anyway. I grew curious about this topic and did some research. I came across the CDC screen time recommendations for babies and it stated (in 2019) that children under the age of 2 should not have any screen time except for an occasional video call. Shockingly, I just checked the CDC website (2023) and they have lowered the age for screen time from 2 years old to 18 months.

Some people might not understand how to keep their children entertained without screens, but it is possible. Children who are not used to having a screen plopped in front of them usually find ways to entertain themselves. For our boys, they usually find toys or books to play with that I have available. Sometimes they even create their own games to play with each other and I honestly don't think that would happen if they were preoccupied watching something. We allow them to be slightly bored, and that enhances their creativity.

Not allowing children to have screen time gets increasingly more difficult the more time you spend away from home. When we go out to a restaurant or a relative's house, we have to prepare ourselves. This is usually when we become frustrated because the boys are excited and want to run and explore in the new environment that they are not used to. When we are able to prepare ourselves, I will usually pack some books, small toys, or paper and washable crayons. These items keep them busy for a while before we have to get them moving again. Sometimes we have to take them walking outside just to get their wiggles out, and then we go back in to join our family. We do make sacrifices because we are adamant that they will not have screen time yet, but we truly feel it will be worth it. I know some people say children learn a lot through the shows they watch, and maybe they do, but I would rather try to teach them those things myself, and through books.

If you are leaning towards not allowing your child to have screen time, this should also make you more mindful of how often you are preoccupied with a screen. In 2019, the CDC recommended that adults have no more than 2 hours of screen time per day. Screen time includes TV, phones, video games, or computers. When I recently checked what the CDC recommends for adults in 2023, I couldn't find a recommendation! Now that so many people spend time working in front of a screen, it's really difficult to limit it. However, we can limit how much TV we watch and how often we spend scrolling through our phones. If you don't want your child to be an addict who needs a screen in order to function, then try your best to lessen your own screen time. You will be happier and healthier for it. Benefits of less screen time include having more physical activity, better social connections, less anxiety, and better sleep.

We recently told one of our acquaintances that our boys had never watched TV or shows on our phone, and she was amazed. She said our boys were lucky to have each other because they can play together, but she felt like she had to show her child TV when she was busy cooking and doing household things. I do agree that it is easier when you have multiples because they can entertain each other, but it is still possible to not have screen time with one child. If they are not used to watching shows, they will find ways to entertain themselves, and that will increase their creativity. You can also invest in a learning tower for their 1st birthday and then they can "help" you while you're cooking!

Books I recommend for babies & toddlers:

- Leslie Patricelli Books

- Lovevery Books

- Baby Bath Books

- Winnie the Pooh Books

- Pete the Kitty or Pete the Cat Books

- Construction Site Series - Sherri Rinker

- Chris Ferrie Baby Science Books

YouTube Video I recommend for learning about less screen time:

- Addiction to Technology is Ruining Lives - Simon Sinek on Inside Quest by Andre White

7: Healthy Eating for Your Family

As I mentioned previously, I try to live life in the most natural way - at least with what I have the capacity for. My husband and I do our best to live healthy lives, and were initially influenced by the Blue Zones lifestyle. Blue Zones are different areas around the world where individuals live to be 100 years old without any illnesses such as diabetes, high blood pressure, or cancer. When I learned about these people, I wanted to do what they were doing. I never want to live a lifestyle that can lead me to sickness and negatively impact my family. After some research, we realized a plant-based diet was one of the healthiest ways to eat. Not only is this diet good for your health, it is also great if you love animals and want to protect our Earth. At first, we were a little confused on how not eating meat or consuming dairy products would help our Earth, but if you do some research, you will find that it is true.

I live in a predominantly Hispanic community where there is meat in every meal; breakfast, lunch, and dinner are not complete without meat. When we learned that red meat is literally a carcinogen (a cancer-causing agent), and realized we were not eating nearly enough fruits and veggies, we were shocked. I usually tell people from my hometown, "If you're not plant-based, you're probably animal-based." My husband and I both lost weight when we stopped eating meat. It was something we didn't expect to happen, but we were happily surprised when it did. About a year later, we decided to take the plunge into a full vegan diet and stopped eating eggs, cheese, and all dairy products. When we did this, we lost even more weight, which really caught me off guard because I had just delivered two babies! Overall, we felt strong, happy, and healthy with the way we were eating and we definitely wanted our children to have this diet as well.

When we told our pediatrician that we wanted to raise our children on a vegan diet, he did not think it would work out and was a little negative about it. My husband would say, "He's going to tell us something about giving our children fruits and vegetables, but does he say anything to the meat-eating families who give their children fast food?" It was something we felt strongly about, and we've never had any difficulties with it. Our boys are thriving on a vegan diet and always have more than enough energy from their food to get them through the day. Our boys are also never constipated, as we hear some other babies are.

I know it's really difficult for working parents to buy, make, and prepare food for every single meal, but it can be done. Our boys started eating solids at 6 months because we waited for them to be able to sit up on their own. We had learned a saying that said "Food before 1 is just for fun," so we kept that in mind. We would only give them a little bit of peanut butter, smashed veggies/fruit, and bland oatmeal in the beginning. We slowly worked our way up to oatmeal with cinnamon, veggie soups, and toast with peanut butter.

Our boys stopped drinking soy formula at 13 months, and never had a bottle again after that. We didn't abruptly take it away, we slowly weaned one bottle feeding at a time. After this, we had them on a whole foods diet. They would ask us at the pediatrician's office which milk they drank, and we just said, "None." Our boys were healthy so they couldn't tell us anything.

For their first birthday, we were excited and wanted to buy something for them. We bought a veggie soup from one of our favorite restaurants, and they did not like it. This was the first and last time they had restaurant food until they were about 2. When I tell people this, they are usually shocked, but it's true, our boys did not have a full meal from a restaurant until they were a little over 2 years old. Once they started eating more of a variety of food with different flavors, we allowed ourselves to eat out about once or twice a week in order to stay healthy and save money.

When it comes to birthday parties and Halloween, many parents might feel conflicted about giving their child sweets. If you are truly okay with your child having sugary foods, then you have nothing to worry about. If you are weary about it, and you know you would rather your child not consume candy, then don't be shy about it. When we go to birthday parties, we clearly tell our family and friends that we do not want our children to consume animal products or candies. We get pushback at times, but they are our children and we want to help them build healthy habits.

This past Halloween, there was a trick-or-treating event at the library, and I simply walked the boys out when they began passing out candy. I know some people may find this extreme, but we are very mindful with what we allow our boys to eat. If they do not know something, they will not crave it or miss it. Therefore, if they do not know candy, they will not ask for it. Ultimately, you are in control of what your child consumes. Don't let anyone guilt trip you into feeding them a certain way just because everyone else does it.

Easy Meals You Can Prepare

My husband and I were both working full time from the time the boys were 3 months until they were about 2-and-a-half. It was difficult for me to prepare meals during the weekend, but I always got it done. If you feel like you can't do it, I'm here to tell you that you can! It is exhausting, but it is rewarding when you can say you work hard to provide and prepare healthy meals for your family.

When I was working, I would prepare about 14 jars of overnight oats for the week. I still do this even now that I am not working. I would take one jar for lunch with me every day, the boys would share one for breakfast every day, and my husband would take one for breakfast with him when he worked. Vegan overnight oats are honestly so delicious, healthy, and easy to make. It's also great that they last all week in the fridge! All we would do the morning of is top the oats with fresh fruit, and it was good to go!

Beans and granola are two other staples we have in our household. There is a delicious granola recipe we use from the Blue Zones Solutions book, and we either use it to top our smoothies with, or eat it as a cereal with bananas. Beans are full of carbs and protein; they will give you the strength and energy that you need in your busy life. Our boys will often have bean toast, tostadas, or tacos for dinner. My husband loves to eat tostadas, and I love that it's a very easy dinner we just top with beans, tomatoes, spinach, and avocado.

Recently, we've been having smoothies every day for breakfast, and they are so delicious and filling. We make a large amount and have enough so we can save some for our boys for the following day. Smoothies are a little harder to make when you're busy because they're not something you meal prep for the week, but if you have 30 extra minutes in the morning, they are great for breakfast! We try to diversify the plants we consume, so we switch it up between the following smoothies: blueberry, mango/pineapple, acai, dragon fruit, celery, papaya, beet, etc. Most of our smoothies are based with bananas, so we always have frozen bananas in the freezer.

If you're interested in making meal planning work for you, I suggest getting organized about it. When I was working, every week I would write my grocery list for the following week on

Wednesday or Thursday. I would schedule to pick up the groceries as a curbside order on Fridays so I would have all the ingredients ready for the weekend. On Saturday mornings I would still wake up at 5 AM to begin meal prepping. I would prioritize oats first because that was a constant. Then, I would make another large meal for the week while the boys were taking their nap (usually a pot of vegan chili or lentil soup). If we were low on granola, I would either do that on Saturday night, or Sunday morning.

Mealtime Struggles

From the time the boys were 18 months to about 2-and-a-half, meal times were my least favorite times of day. They would get messy beyond belief and began to reject food at times. I know this is normal for children at that age, but I found it so frustrating. They had gotten into the routine of having their main course and then fruit for dessert, so when they began to not want their main course, we told them they could not have their fruit unless they finished their meal. This worked most of the time, and at times that I felt we overserved them, I would allow them to have their fruit anyway.

There were a handful of days when they were adamant they did not want what I had served for them, and they went without eating that meal. I was worried when that happened, but I also sometimes don't feel like eating dinner, so I figured it was fine. Now, in order to prevent pushback, I try to give them options. "Do you want bean tacos or bean tostadas?" "Do you want oats or PB&J?" This has been a big help and we've seen them rejecting food less often. If I truly do not have much to offer them, I will explain to them that they only have one option, and if they do not eat, I just make sure they eat their next meal.

Many times when we are eating with family, they tell us our boys are great eaters. It hadn't occurred to me that a toddler could be a bad eater or reject the majority of their meals. One of the things that allows our boys to fully indulge during meal times is that they are hungry. They only have breakfast, lunch, and dinner so their stomachs are empty and ready to be filled by the time we sit down for a meal. I will occasionally give them a snack if I know a meal will be pushed back because I do not want them to be hungry. However, I think it's good to go easy on the snacks so they are able to eat a full meal when it's time.

Cleaning up after meals was one thing I struggled with when the boys began making a mess. I know it's not something that should be a big deal, but I truly couldn't believe how messy they could be. Now, it's just part of the routine; we clean and vacuum the kitchen every day. It is exhausting, but it is something that just has to be done. If you struggle with this, put on some music and make the most of it. We recently upgraded to a floor vacuum that has a built-in mop, and I love it. The floor used to be sticky all week until I would mop, but now it's clean almost every day. Things like this are worth investing in when you have little ones.

If you decide to use a child-size table for your child to eat at, you can begin at 18 months. We switched to a small table when our boys were 2 years old. When we made this transition, we had to constantly remind them to sit down when they eat. If you lead by example, this process should go very well. We loved not having them in a high chair because they were able to place their dirty bowls in the sink on their own and get their fruit bowls without us having to do it for them. Teaching them this independence is difficult at first, but it is important.

Healthy eating books I recommend:

- Blue Zones Solution - Dan Buettner

- You can also watch the Netflix series instead of reading the book, but the book has good recipes as well.

YouTubers I recommend for healthy smoothie & meal recipes:

- Pick Up Limes

- Fully Raw Kristina

8: The Importance of Nature & Being a Wild Child

Over the years, I've heard and read that being in nature is extremely beneficial. As I got older, and started to become more mindful of the things that brought me happiness, I realized the days I spent outside were my happiest days. During the pandemic, many people stressed how important it was to get outside in order to de-stress, even if it was just for 5 minutes. Because of all of these things, I knew I wanted to have our children outside as often as possible. I had also read how children had better immune systems when they spent more time outside.

By the time our boys were 3 months, my husband and I started taking walks with them in our Baby K'tan's. We even picked up trash one time because the park was filthy, and now they love to pick up trash! I really feel like they have some remembrance of that day and that's why they love to do it. They would prefer picking up water bottles over going down slides any day.

By the time the boys were 5 months, we were using our double stroller every day. We would try to take them on an hour-long walk in the mornings. The evenings were sometimes difficult because we live in South Texas where it easily reaches 100 degrees on any afternoon from May through October. When this happened, we would find a shaded basketball court and walk in circles around it. We try to not let the weather stop us from enjoying nature. During the winter, we take advantage of mid-day walks. We aren't used to the cold, but we still try to bundle up and go outside regardless. We find that no matter the weather, we always come back feeling happy and refreshed after some time outside.

While we are outside, we point out the beauty in the sky, clouds, trees, and animals. We want our boys to have a love and respect for nature, and we see that forming in them every day. We want them to be adventurous and brave, and we feel that our time at playgrounds and nature trails will help them acquire that. Not only is outside time beneficial, but it can help you connect with other parents and children in your neighborhood. We have many close friends whom we've met at the park, and we are so grateful for their friendships and quality time spent with them outside.

As your child gets older, you will realize how difficult it is for them to just sit still and not break anything around the house. No child is meant to sit still, and all children are born with a sense of awe and wonder about their surroundings. This is why it is best to have a good amount of outside time. We love taking our boys to a playground and letting them run wild, it's what's natural to them. It is intimidating to take them outside so much when you think about their safety, but if you teach them that they need to hold your hand, or that they must stay away from the street, they will learn. It takes some time, practice, and patience to do these things, but they are worth it.

Sometimes my boys are screaming wildly while running around the house and giving rough bear hugs, and I tell them, "You all are crazy babies!" To which they respond, "No, wild child!" I love this reminder because it is true. They are wild and good hearted and I want them to be wild and explore for as long as they can. We have taught them when to be disciplined and when they can be wild. Any child can learn this and it's a fun and rewarding process. I highly suggest having outside time as a part of your daily routine.

Even if it's a 5-minute walk to the mailbox, or a quick meal outside; any outside time appreciating nature around you is a gift to be shared with your children.

9: How to Find Happiness

Strong Marriage

Before getting married and having kids, I sporadically heard that having a baby could put a strain on a marriage. I saw it in a few couples around me, but they stayed together, and again I thought, "Then having kids can't be too bad". When we had our twins, we didn't feel a sudden change in our marriage, and we continued to be a strong couple. I saw some indifference when my husband would see me breastfeeding because I literally had to share my body with our babies, but we were still good.

My husband and I are good at communicating and our marriage has been able to persevere. I noticed a slight shift in our marriage when the boys were in their two's, after I started to stay home with them. This might have been psychological for me, as I felt like I didn't have a life and was just living off of my husband. Once I started staying home, all of my time and effort was going to our children and I felt I had little time for my husband. When I did have time, I felt like I didn't have the energy to talk to him, let alone be intimate with him.

There are multiple studies that have been done on how a child can affect your marriage. There is even proof of higher divorce rates for couples who do have children.

The good thing is, just like working at being a good parent, you can also work at being a good spouse. However, I'm here to tell you that children do put a strain on your relationship, and they will do so throughout their entire life. If your children are your world, then you and your partner will continuously have to make adjustments and choices based on their well-being. It is important to always discuss things with your partner before you discuss them with your children.

Your children will hopefully leave you one day when they make their own lives for themselves, but your partner will be the one who stays with you into old age when the children are gone. So, if you see that your relationship is shaky, make efforts to strengthen it. Find time to go on a date no matter how hard it is to leave the kids or find a sitter, it will be worth it.

My husband and I have 2 tips when it comes to marriage advice:

1. Always communicate. If an argument is happening, it is usually because you didn't communicate properly, your spouse didn't communicate properly, or there was a lack of communication coming from both sides. Always remember that you chose your spouse; you love your spouse. You do not want to go through the pain of mistreating them or doing them wrong. In difficult times, express your love and communicate effectively.

2. Put your money together. Having your money together can help you and your spouse set goals together and make you an even stronger couple. When you get married, you start to live and build a life together. For us, this meant paying off student loans together, saving up for our first house together, starting a savings account for our children together, investing together, etc. Having your money together allows a marriage to have clarity and truth, which is what every marriage should have. Put your money together so you can make your marriage stronger and reach your goals together.

Bonus Tip: **Get off of social media**. My husband and I often forget that social media has negative effects on relationships because we've really never had it throughout our marriage. When we first started dating, we were both on a few social media platforms. When we got serious as a couple, we realized it was best if we didn't have social media and deleted our accounts. This made us better as a couple, and better as humans.

Since then, we don't have the temptation to be mindlessly scrolling through our phones, or the temptations of flirting with other people. Now, we only have incognito accounts, together, just so we can search our favorite artists or local pages from time to time, but it causes absolutely no stress or harm to our marriage. I just created an Instagram account in order to promote this book, but my husband has full access to it and I usually only log into it through our desktop.

I highly recommend you and your spouse read Gary Chapman's, "The Five Love Languages", as it will help both of you meet each other's needs and check in with each other when things are rocky in your relationship. For the ladies reading this, I recommend Elizabeth Gilbert's, "City of Girls" when you need motivation to be intimate. Let's be real, parenting is exhausting and you are not always in the mood nor do you have the energy to be intimate. If you need a little push, this book will definitely put you in the mood, and it's just a fun book to get your mind off of parenting.

Happiness of Parents & Children

It has long been known that if parents are happy as a couple, then their children are more likely to be happy as well. I've seen this first hand with my family. My husband and I don't argue often, but on one occasion we did, and I saw it instantly affect our boys. This was surprising to me as our boys were only a little over 2-years-old. My husband and I were having a serious discussion about something and my husband raised his voice slightly (which he usually never does), and one of our boys quickly looked up at him, and then at me. I felt instant regret at the moment and decided to drop the entire discussion until the boys went to sleep. The air in the room was tense and definitely not fun.

On many other occasions, my husband and I will be giddy with each other and playing around. Our boys often look at us in awe because they think we might be fighting, but when they see our laughter and when we invite them to join in on the fun, they are put in such a good mood. If parents are happy, then their children are more likely to be happy.

If you are a single parent or on your own most of the time, then you have to find ways to make yourself happy. When I find myself in a funk and I'm alone with the boys, I put on some happy/positive music and force myself into a good mood. This doesn't always work, but it does most of the time. I also remind myself to be grateful for things around me. If my boys are giving me a hard time, I will say out loud, "I'm so grateful for this day that we have together. I'm grateful for our health. I'm grateful for this food. I'm grateful for my patience." Even if I'm not patient at the time, I try to manifest it. Again, if you are happy, your children are more likely to be happy. Get happy, be happy, stay happy.

Parenting Breaks

If you find that you are unhappy and in a deep funk, it's okay. Try to find what is making you feel that way. It might be that you don't spend enough time with your spouse or your children. Maybe you don't spend enough time by yourself. Whatever it is, pinpoint where your sadness is coming from, and do something to fix it.

For me, I know that my priority is my husband and my children, but I cannot fill their cups unless my cup is full. Therefore, I still wake up at 5 AM most mornings even though I'm not working at a full-time job. I do this so I can get myself ready, do a short workout, drink coffee, read, and prepare a meal all before the boys wake up. Sometimes my morning ritual isn't enough to satisfy me, so I ask my husband for a break. If he can take the boys to the park for just one hour while I have peace and quiet, doing whatever I'd like (usually preparing things for our family), it makes the world of a difference. I am the nicest and happiest mom and wife when they get back.

Similarly, my husband will take breaks as needed. I jokingly tell him that going to work is a break because he doesn't have to deal with two toddlers all day, but it's obviously not a break. When he's not at work, he takes his own breaks by working out and hanging out with his friends when he can. He even took an out-of-country trip recently to visit his best friend. I know I can do the same if I ever want or need to. It's good to give each other space and have parenting breaks.

Don't feel guilty asking for a parenting break because it is difficult to be with little humans all day, every day. You may need time to yourself, or time with a friend to have an adult conversation. You may need time to go buy yourself an outfit that will make you feel good, or maybe you just need time to take a nap! Whatever it is, communicate with those around you so you can get the break that you need. Again, happy parents, happy children.

Books I recommend in this chapter & for happiness:

- The Five Love Languages - Gary Chapman

- City of Girls - Elizabeth Gilbert

- Blue Zones of Happiness - Dan Buettner

10: Working Parents vs. Stay-at-Home Parents

Why I decided to Stay Home

When our twins were 2 months old, we realized that being tired was the new normal, but we were still pretty happy. Our boys were adorable and we learned that babies bring a new, deeper kind of love no one else can give you. We got comfortable with me being home all the time after their birth. I contemplated quitting work before I had to go back after twelve weeks, but we'd never thought about doing that before, so it was too foreign for us to act on it at the time.

I mentioned the idea of staying home with the boys to my mom, but she told me it was good to be a working mom so my children could see that I could support the family as well. I agreed to a certain extent, but going back to work full time still didn't sit right with me. We had (and still have) an abundance of help from our parents, siblings, and friends. We are truly grateful for them as they've made this experience much easier. They allowed us to not have our boys in daycare for the first 2 years that I continued to work.

Before having children, most full-time working parents say they will simply put their child in daycare after their maternity/paternity leave is up. For us, we decided we would find a way to make it work for the boys to not be in daycare. Because my husband works every three days, we were going to ask my mother-in-law to help on the days my husband had to work. Luckily, my mom decided to retire when our boys were 5 months old, so she was able to watch them most of the time and we didn't have to ask my mother-in-law for specific days off.

I was teaching at the time our boys were born, so when I went back to work, I was only focused on finishing the school year (April & May). I kept on explaining to my husband that I felt it would be best for me to stay home, but again, that was never in our plan. Both of our moms were never stay at home moms, and we didn't understand families that did that enough for us to do it. Therefore, I told my husband I wanted to get a librarian position as I had just received my Masters in Library Science. I kept on telling myself, and my husband, that I would quit my teaching job if I didn't get a librarian position.

Right away, a librarian position opened up in my school district, so I applied. I got the job, and it was back to work for me after summer break. I was honestly excited for this job. As a new mom, I felt like my life was not my own anymore and I wanted change. I was happy to get the position because it was at an elementary school. I was a high school teacher before, so this was great! This meant that I could take my boys to school with me once they entered kindergarten. I was happy with the change; I would go into work at an earlier time, but I would also get out earlier than I would have as a teacher. Over time, it became difficult for me because I often found myself rushing home after work and constantly wondering how my babies were doing. I liked the job, but I wanted to be with my boys much more than I wanted to be at work.

Towards the end of my first year being an elementary school librarian, I began to realize that I did not approve of the way the children were being taught in a post-pandemic world. All of the students from pre-kinder to fifth grade had electronic devices they used very often, there seemed to be even more testing than before, and there was also very little outdoor or physical activity time the students had. I brought my concerns up to my husband and told him I did not want our children attending public school. I had previously called a Montessori school we have in town and I was planning on sending our boys there. While I did get a good vibe from the school, it didn't sit well with me to send them there either.

My husband and I asked many other parents about their children's education. I brought my concerns up to my best friend, and she said they were discussing homeschooling. We had never thought about doing that as it would mean I would have to be out of work, but we didn't completely shun the idea either. We also heard that one of the private schools in town was very good, and it was within walking distance from our house, so we considered that for a while. I truly wanted to send the boys to a Montessori elementary school, but we have none for children ages 6 - 12 in our city, so I even proposed a plan of moving out of town to my husband; he thought I was crazy.

At the end of all of this back-and-forth, we decided I would stay home to teach our boys at least until they turned 6 years old, and then we could re-evaluate our plans from there. I wanted to complete three years as a librarian because that seemed like a fair amount of time to give the school, and it would help us save up a little more money. However, after a year and a half of working as a full-time librarian and part time mom, I had had enough. I was desperate to spend more time with my husband and children. We decided I would stop working as a librarian after two years, and we have no regrets about our decision.

If You're Considering Staying Home

Whether you are a working parent or a stay-at-home parent, just be sure the decision feels right to you. I never thought I would be a stay-at-home mom, but here I am. I still have trouble with the fact that I do not bring income into the household, but it's okay. We are fortunate enough to be financially stable for me to stay home, and my family and I are all so grateful for that. Some families feel better when the dad stays home, and I'm happy to say we're seeing that more often now. Every family is different, so you just need to do what is right for you. Most mornings after my boys wake up, I go to their rooms and we give each other long hugs, kisses, and happily tell each other good morning. I often think, "If I was at work right now, I'd be missing this." Staying home is a challenge at times, but it is extremely worth it.

I often tell other moms that working part time is probably the best. Being at home with your children full time can be emotionally and physically exhausting, so it can be good to have a place to go that gives you another purpose. Personally, I did not find any part-time librarian positions. I also needed a job with a flexible schedule. With my husband's work schedule, it's difficult for me to have a set time to work, so now I just write whenever I can! If you can find a part-time job or a hobby that can make you money and give you a break from the kids, I'd say that's a win-win.

When I decided to stay home with my boys, I felt like an outcast. I was surrounded by working moms in my family and at work. I was honestly embarrassed to tell some of them I had decided to stay home with my boys. If you feel like that, it's okay, just be sure you are happy with your decision. Every family takes a different path that works for them.

If you feel like you want to stay home, but can't because you've already put too much effort into your schoolings and career, I feel you. Women in the U.S. are so lucky to have access to education and careers unlike women in other parts of the world. It is not something we should take for granted, or simply throw away. However, it is something we can definitely put on hold. Many people may think, "She has a degree and she's not using it for anything." However, just because someone is not using their degree at the moment, doesn't mean they will never use it. Additionally, moms who are educated can better educate their children. Once the time is right, stay-at-home parents can go back to work at any time they choose, and that is the beauty of it.

If you ultimately decide to stay home, be prepared to force yourself to slow down. Babies and toddlers live a slow life and do not like to be rushed. When I first stopped working, I found myself rushing my boys when they were brushing their teeth or putting on their clothes. At some point I thought, "What's the rush? We have time to enjoy every moment." Once you stay home, you may also feel a little lost on what to do. I honestly sometimes feel like I have impostor syndrome. I think, "Who let me be a mom?" but after some time you get used to it being your full-time job. The transition is difficult if and when you stop working, but if you stay home with them as soon as they're born, the attachment to your child will likely be strong from the beginning.

Family Values & Schooling

When you have your first child, they make you re-evaluate every-thing you believe is right in the world. My husband and I are really good at seeing things from a blank slate, so as much as we value the beliefs our parents instilled in us, we still try to think independently as well. He and I can go back-and-forth on certain topics for a long time. We usually come to a consensus together, but sometimes we don't. When it comes to raising children together, it is important that you and your spouse are in agreement.

We know our family values are to not eat animals, keep education and nature of high importance, and be a good person. We knew that the real world would not cater to our vegan children, and that was one thing we knew we would have to take control of. I envisioned myself packing lunch for our boys even in their pre-K days, so that wasn't the main reason we decided to homeschool, but because of our diet, we feel more comfortable having them home. When it comes to nature and education being important, for us, that means having minimal screen time. As I mentioned earlier, at the public school I was working at, I saw an abundance of screen time and minimal time spent outside. Because of this, we were eventually adamant on homeschooling.

Some parents have their child's first 18 years of education planned out before the baby is even born. I was kind of like this, but the truth is, you honestly never know and you just need to decide as you go. As I mentioned earlier, I was excited to take my boys with me to public elementary school when they were of age. I had no idea how uncomfortable I would be with it in a post pandemic world though.

Even now, people ask me how long we will homeschool, and I tell them I truly don't know. Some days I feel like I can't be home with them one more day and I'm ready to enroll them in a preschool. Other days, I want to homeschool them until they're college ready. I've learned to just go with what is best for our boys at the moment, and what's best for their future. I know the first six years of their life are vital, so I truly do want to keep them home until that age. However, if I feel like I am not giving them the best care and education at home, then I will definitely do my research and decide which other options are best for them.

Every family is going to have a different schooling path. Don't feel pressured to do what everyone else is doing, and don't be afraid to change your plan. You are capable of deciding what school is best for your children, and you will be able to make it happen. Finalize what your family values are and make sure their schooling reflects that well.

Getting Your Finances in Order

When I was leaving my job, many of my coworkers would say, "You're so lucky to stay home," but the truth is, many people can stay home! A lot of the ladies who would tell me that have husbands with the same, or similar jobs to my husband. So, if we can do it, why can't they? It's all about discipline and perspective.

Ever since my husband and I got married, we learned to live off of his paycheck and save all of mine. At first, we saved my check so we could pay off all of our college debt. Then, we saved all of my check so we could save for a house. We had a small hiccup with our savings after we had our boys because we didn't know where to allocate our money after having kids (there's so many options). After we decided I would stay home, for about eight months we made sure we could live off of my husband's check and saved all of mine again.

I know many people have debt, and they work to pay it off, but there are always ways for one parent to stay home. It does mean you have to live more frugally (which I love, and take as a challenge), but it also means more meaningful time with your family. For us, not having new cars and shopping at thrift stores means we can be together more often, and that is worth it. We were going to have to spend about $1,200 every month to send our boys to daycare and have less time with them. Those facts just weren't worth it for us. We are so grateful we made the decision that we did, and the great thing is, it's not permanent! I know I can go back to work whenever I want, but right now, we like that I am our children's main teacher and guide.

Find out what is best for your family, and make it happen. Anything is possible, and nothing has to be permanent if you don't want it to be. If you're looking to stay home and want to know where you can save money, I suggest the following:

- Look at your credit cards and checking account to actually see what you spend money on. For most people, their largest chunks of money go to housing and cars. If you can downsize or get fully-functioning used cars, I highly suggest that. You can save thousands of dollars a year just by trading in your cars for more affordable ones.

- If you can get rid of your car payments and only have a housing payment, that means you can likely live off of one income.

- We save a lot of money by cleaning our own house and cutting our own grass. Most of our housework is DIY.

- We personally thought solar panels were going to be more affordable than our regular light bill, so we made that change as well. Do the math to see if that will save you money.

- At the grocery store, we always look for coupons and buy the most affordable option of what we are looking for.

- Our cell phones are not new, but they work and we don't owe any money on them, so our monthly bill is very low.

- We only eat out once or twice a week, so we spend no more than $250.00 on eating out every month.

- We try our best to be frugal, but intentional, with the gifts we give and the purchases we make.

- We try not to spend unless it's absolutely necessary. If I really want something, I see if I can ask for it for my birthday or Christmas.

- We don't spend on expensive haircuts or trips to the salon. My husband only goes when there is a special occasion, usually every two months, if not he cuts his own hair. I get a haircut about once a year, and I go with someone who charges $8!

- We don't have gym memberships. Our friends' gyms and YouTube videos have kept us fit so far.

- We have minimal streaming subscriptions (only two).

- We only spend money on necessities. If we need to make a large purchase, we are sure to save up for it and do our research on when the best time is to purchase the item.

- I rarely go out shopping, and if I do, it's usually to the thrift store.

- We always take the time to shop around for the most affordable car, home, and life insurance as those can be pricey.

If you have absolutely no knowledge or minimal knowledge of how to take charge of your finances, I recommend Dave Ramsey. He can teach you how to snowball and work your way out of debt while saving money. If you have that knowledge already, then I recommend looking into financial freedom podcasts and books. Even if you decide to continue working, it is good to learn how to live off of one income. You can have the second income used for savings or vacation money.

Books I recommend to get yourself in a better financial situation:

- The Latte Factor - David Bach

- Your Money or Your Life - Vicki Robbin & Joe Dominguez

- I Will Teach You to Be Rich - Ramit Sethi

- The Simple Path to Wealth - J.L. Collins

Documentary I recommend to get yourself in a better financial situation:

- Playing with FIRE: The Documentary

11: Life With a 2-Year-Old

Potty Training

Right before our boys turned 2, I decided I wanted to try to potty train them. It was right before I had to go back to work from my winter break and I wanted to get it over with. I had heard that cloth-diapered babies were easier to potty train, so I figured it wouldn't be too bad. I asked my best friend how she did it and she sent me a YouTube video for how to potty train a little boy in 3 days.

I am writing this 9 months after my first attempt to potty train our boys, and I still remember how horrible it was. First of all, it was like having newborns again. We couldn't go anywhere because we didn't want to put a diaper on them, so we were stuck at home all day. We were constantly cleaning up after them and getting frustrated when they just couldn't hold it. I know it's insane how quickly we expect our children to learn how to relieve themselves in a toilet when they have been going in a diaper their entire life. However, when you are constantly cleaning up pee off the floor, it just puts you in a sour mood.

After about a month, we were comfortable taking our boys out and about, but we had to take them to pee every 15 minutes if we didn't want them to have an accident. It was exhausting. After about four months, they were able to hold it a little longer, but we still took them potty every 30 minutes. Luckily, they always told us when they had to poop, but we wouldn't know about them having to pee until it was already on their shorts. Now, 9 months after our initial potty-training date, they can hold it for about 1 hour and they are napping in their undies. We feel like we've made tons of progress, and we are so grateful it only gets better every day.

I wanted to write about this to let parents know that it is hard. Other sources don't say it's hard, they usually say something along the lines of, "Be patient, don't show them anger." It is true that you need to be patient, but it's not true that you can potty train overnight. It is a long process. I suggest, if you want to have your child potty trained by 2, start when they are 18 months. Children's sensitive period for pottying is 18 - 24 months. Take your time introducing them to the potty, showing them how to go potty, and encouraging them to go often. After 6 months, I'm sure they will get the hang of it. They are more aware than you may believe.

I remember a few weeks after we began potty training, our pediatrician asked how it was going, and I told him, "It's the hardest thing I've ever had to do in my life," to which he replied, "Well you must have a very good life." He's not wrong, but I was just being truthful. I don't want to sound negative, but I do want to be honest. I just can't believe people don't talk about how difficult these things are. Many people say girls are easier to potty train than boys. If that's the truth, then don't take this so seriously if you're the parent of a girl.

We taught our boys to go in the little potty first and then transitioned them to the toilet, but you can go straight to the toilet right away if you feel that will work. Having a little potty to take on the go was very helpful to us as we would just have our boys go in the car. Many times parks do not have restrooms, and if they do, they may not be clean. I recommend having a little potty in the car as it is helpful for public outings. I know it's gross, but we usually just dump the pee out on the grass somewhere (dogs do it too). Luckily, our boys have never pooped in their little potty, but I suggest having a plastic bag in the car in case they do need to poop, you can place the bag inside the potty to catch the poop.

Elimination Communication

When I was pregnant, I heard of something called elimination communication. I read a book about it, but it seemed way too hippie for me (and I'm pretty hippie-ish). At first, I just thought of elimination communication as an early form of potty training, which is essentially what it is. When I read a book about it though, it said to never have your baby in a diaper, to which I soon stopped reading the book. When our boys were about 18 months, my friend Raquel told me she was doing elimination communication with her newborn along with cloth diapers. She made it seem so do-able! She would have the cloth diaper on her baby at all times, but right after every feeding, she would take her baby to the toilet. Now, her baby is only 18 months and she's almost fully potty trained! I definitely want to try this with our next baby.

The trick is to get them used to going in the toilet when they can, but if they go in their diaper, that's okay too. I later heard an Ellen Fisher podcast episode with Alicia Silverstone, and she also made it sound so simple. What she said really struck me. She mentions how we literally train our babies to go potty in a diaper when we can just train them to go in a toilet from the get-go. Many parents who do elimination communication have babies who only poop in the toilet by the time they are 12 months. This is awesome! It can't hurt holding them over the toilet for 2 minutes after every feeding. As with everything else, do what is best for you and your family. Nothing is one-size-fits-all.

Frustration & Respectful Parenting

Everyone has heard the term "terrible twos". In the respectful parenting realm, they all ignore this term and usually say the child is simply misunderstood, which is true. I think it might be called terrible twos because it makes the parents feel terrible. Right before our boys turned 2, we noticed they wanted more independence. We tried to give them their freedom by teaching them to do things how we wanted them to be done, and then allowing them to complete those tasks on their own. It worked out overall, but sometimes a 2-year-old just catches you off guard with their frustrations. You can ask them to do something so simple, for example, "Can you please pick up the orange you dropped?", and they respond with a firm, "No," and a sly smile on their face.

It's really surprising to parents when their sweet baby now has full blown tantrums over something so small. This is when I started to lose my shit as a parent. I was so torn. I love my babies so much, but they were driving me insane. Part of it was fear that I was raising disrespectful children. When I looked around at the park and public library, I noticed that all 2-year-olds did this. Their parents ask them to do something, and it seems like the only word they know is, "No."

When this happens now, I learn to just smile and not take it seriously. I usually have to stop what I'm doing, go up to my child, look them in the eyes and ask them to look at me as well (which can take another minute to get them to do). Then, I proceed to explain to them why I need them to do something, and I ask them nicely to do it again. This will usually work; if it doesn't work, I will repeat the process, but then add that there will be a consequence if they don't do what I am asking.

Many places that give parenting advice will suggest to acknowledge their feelings when they are being set in their ways. For example, if my son does not want to put the magnet tiles away because we are going to go for a walk, I will tell him, "I know you really want to keep playing with the magnet tiles right now, but didn't you want to see the diggers on our walk? Would you like 2 more minutes?" To which he will usually agree. It is good to empathize with them and it does work most times. For the times it doesn't work, try your best to stay calm and explain to them when they settle down. I used to say I wanted to be a mediator, and now I feel like I am one every day. I am constantly, carefully negotiating with a 2-year-old so they do not commit an act of rage on me. It is what it is, and all we can do is try our best. They have a lot of feelings, and we need to teach them how to cope with them.

When we know there is going to be a transition, we try our best to warn them so they're not caught off guard. We will tell them, "In 2 minutes we're going to clean up so we can wash our hands and eat dinner." We will then repeat that phrase when there is 1 minute left and sometimes even 30 seconds. This has been pretty helpful for us. We also try to give them choices, and they usually like that. For example, if one of my boys has a toy and my other son wants it, I will tell them, "In 1 minute, we're going to switch toys." Then, after one minute I tell my first son, "Are you going to give the toy to your brother, or should mama help you?" They usually want to do it on their own, and if they don't, I'll help them. This may or may not result in a tantrum.

It is best practice to offer them choices when you can. If you are going somewhere and they're not ready to get dressed, you can give them two options. Do you want the red shoes, or the black shoes? Do you want to open the door, or do I do it? Would you like to help me carry the keys, or would you like to carry your book? These little things really do go a long way.

All of this took a lot of practice and energy from me and my husband. When our boys turned 2, I had to write little notes all over our house that said, "Show Respect and Teach Independence." I just needed the reminder. It was so easy to get frustrated with them, but I wanted them to treat me with respect, so I had to treat them with respect. We also used to ignore their tantrums, but that's never good. We try our best to relate to them now. If they are being unreasonable to the point of no return, I take them to a room where we can be alone with no distractions. I offer them a hug and remind them to breathe. I want them to learn how to calm themselves down as it can be a worthy lifelong tool. If they do not want to breathe, I simply tell them we will not leave the room until they do so.

One time, out of nowhere, one of my sons had a meltdown over us having lunch. My husband and I were so hungry and honestly didn't want to deal with it. I took our son into our room, offered him a hug, asked him to breathe, and then asked him why he was crying. He told me, "No oats." He didn't want to eat overnight oats, but I had already prepared them and did not have the energy to prepare anything else. I told him, "What if we add something to your oats? Would you like to add raspberries or raisins?" He happily said he wanted raisins. I reminded him that I loved him, and we went to eat as if nothing happened even though he was full blown crying and screaming 4 minutes before. When I came back from talking with him, my husband was astonished and told me I was amazing.

Respectful parenting takes a lot of time and energy, but it is possible and it is worth it. If you have a bad moment as a parent, don't be too hard on yourself; no one is perfect. I was walking with one of my friends the other day and we were discussing how difficult 2-year-olds can be. I told her I've thankfully learned to be calmer with them and that it takes practice. To which she told me, "But sometimes we still scream at them because we just can't do it anymore." I was so shocked to hear her say this out loud. Most parents don't admit that they even raise their voice at their children. I looked at her and said, "Yes! It's horrible. Why do they bring out the worst in us? I never used to have anger issues and I would never do that to anyone else." She said, "Children know how to push your limits, and they don't know how or when to stop like adults do." She's right, and we have to be adult enough to handle the situation appropriately. Sadly, sometimes we don't have the capacity to do so.

During the process of writing this book, I had one really bad evening with my boys. It was like I had a parent tantrum and I couldn't believe it. My husband wasn't home, and it was the result of frustration, exhaustion, and anxiety all in one. I raised my voice at the boys multiple times that night. I felt like such a horrible mother and apologized to them right away. I literally didn't know what to do with myself afterwards. I felt embarrassed even though no one but my boys saw me like that. I literally kept asking myself, "How could I be such a horrible mother?"

The next morning while I was having coffee with my husband, I told him everything that happened and I couldn't stop crying. My husband is always so calm and understanding and he reminded me that our boys can be frustrating, and that I am doing a great job despite that moment. I honestly just think I needed to recharge that day because I continued to cry and be slightly agitated with the boys throughout the morning. My husband took them out of the house for a couple of hours so I could have my space. When they came back home for lunch, I was a completely different person. I was so glad my husband saw me like that and gave me space, because we all need that as parents. Ever since then, he's realized he can make the world of a difference if he takes the boys for 2 hours every once in a while so I can have some alone time.

If you have an outburst at your kids, or you do something you're not proud of as a parent, it's okay. You are not defined by the worst thing you've done. Every day is a new day. Every moment is a new moment that you can start out fresh. If you have a slip up in the morning, it's okay. Apologize to your kids and tell them (and yourself) that you're going to do better throughout the day. No one is perfect. It is good for us to show our children that we are only human and we make mistakes, but we learn from those mistakes in order to make ourselves better.

Teaching Independence

By the age of 2, your child should begin to do certain things independently. Some parents begin to teach their children these things at the age of 1. I think it's best to look for cues on when your child is ready, and do your best to teach them how they can function independently throughout their day. When you do ask them to do something, be sure to ask it in a respectful way, as if you were asking your spouse. Here are a few things you can allow them to become independent with:

- Cleaning up their toys: I have been teaching our boys how to put their toys away since they were 6 months old. I would place all the toys in their basket and say, "Mama's cleaning up." Around 9 months, they started to help me do it. Now, I can just say, "Boys, please clean up before we go to grandma's house," and they'll do it quickly with no trouble. If you want a tidy house, this is a habit you should teach your children early on. I also try to stop them from getting a new toy out until their other toys are put away.

- Brushing their teeth: You can allow your child to try to brush their teeth on their own, and then you can offer to "help" them. You will need a stool in the bathroom for this. When you are brushing their teeth, be sure they are focused on what you are doing so they can learn. Explain to them what you are doing so they can do the same next time. We allowed our boys to begin putting their own toothpaste on their toothbrushes at the 2-and-a-half-year mark. They get so excited to do it, it's really cute.

- Putting on their clothes: At the age of 2, our boys started putting their undies and pants on independently. This can be taught earlier as well. You have to teach and show them a couple of times, and then encourage them to do it. After that, they should be able to do it on their own. We also taught them how to put their socks on a little after they turned 2.

- Getting their meal items ready: Once our boys turned 2, we transitioned them out of their high chairs and into a child-sized table. We gave them their own cupboard in the kitchen and taught them how to take their own napkins and utensils to their table. We would place their bowls or plates on the counter and they would carefully get their food and take it to their table. We wanted them to do everything they could possibly do independently.

- Putting dishware in the sink: Once our boys are done with their main course, they place their bowls or plates into the sink and then grab their dessert (fruit) from the counter. You will need a stool in the kitchen for this, and it also helps for washing their hands before and after meals.

- Throwing things in the trash or hamper: We often ask our boys to place things in the trash or hamper for us. We use cloth napkins during mealtimes, so they know to place them in the hamper right after a meal.

- Putting on shoes & jackets: Our boys learned to put their shoes and jackets on independently a couple of months before they turned 3. They have learned how to put their jackets on the Montessori way (by placing it on the floor, putting their arms through the arm holes, and flipping it over their head), but they still need assistance zipping them up. Shoes are something they learned a little later, but some of our nieces learned to put on their shoes at the age of 2!

- Making their bed: Children can learn how to make their bed at 3 or 4 years of age. We don't have traditional sheets for our boys, but sometimes when I go into their rooms after they wake up, they have already placed all the pillows and blankets where they belong. It really pays off for them to see you cleaning and tidying all the time because they will mimic you and the habit will continue.

- Asking them for help whenever you can: Sometimes we are so used to doing things on our own, we forget our children can be helpers. I realized this one time when my husband was out of town and one of my sons was pooping. I knew we were going to be glued to the toilet for a while, but we had just come back from the groceries and the house was a mess. I asked my other son if he could bring me the wipes. He came back and said, "Need anything else, Mama?" So, I took advantage and asked him to throw some things in the trash and some other things in the hamper. I then asked him to go carefully upstairs and bring more jeans because his brother had gotten his wet. He was so helpful and I was astonished. He did everything much slower than I would have, but he did it nonetheless. Once in a while, take time to look around and think about what your kids can help you with. If you need to complete a task and you feel like you can do it with them around, then go for it. Sometimes the boys help me make granola or banana bread on their learning tower. The process takes a little longer than I would like it to, but they have fun.

Books I recommend on Montessori & Respectful Parenting:

- Montessori From the Start - Lillard & Jessen

- How to Raise an Amazing Child the Montessori Way - Tim Seldin

- No Bad Kids: Toddler Discipline without Shame - Janet Lansbury

Podcast I mentioned in this chapter:

- Taboo Parenting and Being Vegan Before It Was Cool with Alicia Silverstone - The Ellen Fisher Podcast

Conclusion: The Truth, Part 2

Parenting is extremely difficult. Parenting is extremely rewarding. There is a roller coaster ride between those two points, and it is one that you do not want to miss. While our children are young, we should do our absolute best to make their lives better than ours have ever been. We should teach them things we never knew, and we should encourage them to be better than we will ever be. Our children are our world and we will make countless sacrifices for their health and happiness.

I know things do not always go your way as a parent, and you may feel very discouraged at times. Doing your best is all you can do. Let your children see your mistakes, so they can see that you learn from them and are able to grow as a person. I know they are a handful when they are babies and toddlers, but enjoy the chaos. Enjoy their cuteness and innocence because they will never be this little again. If you find yourself getting frustrated with them, take the time to hug them and tell them you love them, it will likely make things better.

While you are going through the difficulties of parenthood, don't forget about yourself. If there is a dream or goal that you have, keep going for it. Parenting does not disable you from doing anything. Rather, it enables you to show your children that anything is possible. Yes, we must do what is best for our children, but we must also fulfill our callings. There is always room for children and parents to have their separate happinesses, together. As of now, my personal happiness is being in nature, being with my husband, being with my children, being with my family, and doing a personal creative project (like this book). I do not get to do all of these things every day, but I do my best to prioritize them.

If you are a parent who feels like your life is over because you are tied down with children, you're wrong. Sit down and brainstorm what is best for your children and yourself. There is always a way to accommodate everyone. You must continue to do what makes you happy because 18 years will go by faster than you know, and then you will be left to live with your life decisions on your own. You do not want to have any regrets.

Parenting is fun, purposeful, tiresome, and rewarding. I hope you continue to enjoy the journey of parenthood up until you and your children are of old age. I hope you continue to learn and grow as a person so you can share those things with your children. I hope you and your children never give up on your dreams and on making the world a better place. The journey is long and hard, and oftentimes feels never ending, but there is light every morning, and that gives us hope to carry on. The obstacles will lead you to a life of happiness.

Books I recommend for becoming a better person overall:

- The Four Agreements - Don Miguel Ruiz

- The Art of Living - Thich Nhat Hanh

Acknowledgements:

I could not have written this book without my husband's support. He gave me the space and encouragement I needed to complete it. Thank you to my mom who believes I can be a writer and gets excited with every small idea I have. Thank you to my beautiful children for allowing me to be your mom and go on this journey with you. Thank you to Raquel Brizuela Guzman for looking over this book for me; you are going to be an amazing twin mama.

References:

Ayuob, M. (2021). 5 ways slimming screen time is good for your health. Mayo Clinic Health System. https://www.mayoclinichealthsystem.org/hometown-health/featured-topic/5-ways-slimming-screen-time-is-good-for-your-health

Brittle, Z. (2015). When three's not the charm: How to manage the higher risk of divorce when baby comes along. The Washington Post. https://www.washingtonpost.com/news/inspired-life/wp/2015/06/30/when-threes-not-the-charm-how-to-manage-the-higher-risk-of-divorce-when-baby-comes-along/Montessori, M. (2008). *The Montessori Method* (Centennial, p. 26).

Center for Disease Control and Prevention. (2023). Breastfeeding Benefits Both Baby and Mom. https://www.cdc.gov/nccdphp/dnpao/features/breastfeeding-benefits/index.html#:~:text=Breastfeeding%20can%20help%20protect%20babies,ear%20infections%20and%20stomach%20bugs

Center for Disease Control and Prevention. (2022). Breastfeeding Report Card. https://www.cdc.gov/breastfeeding/data/reportcard.htm#prin

Center for Disease Control and Prevention. (2021). Infants (0-1 year of age). https://www.cdc.gov/ncbddd/

childdevelopment/positiveparenting/infants.
html#:~:text=Limit%20screen%20time.,media%20
other%20than%20video%20chatting

Duffy, A. (2021). Do You Really Save Money Using Cloth
Diapers? Cloth Diapers for Beginners. https://
clothdiapersforbeginners.com/saving-money/
how-much-do-cloth-diapers-cost/#:~:text=This%20
means%2C%20reusable%20diapers%20will,reused%20
on%20your%20next%20child

Gerstein, E. D., et al., (2019). Maternal Depression and Stress
in the Neonatal Intensive Care Unit: Associations With
Mother-Child Interactions at Age 5 Years. *Journal
of the American Academy of Child and Adolescent
Psychiatry*, 58(3), 350–358.e2. https://doi.org/10.1016/j.
jaac.2018.08.016

Ronsmans, C. et. al., (2018). Global epidemiology of use of and
disparities in cesarean sections. *The Lancet*, 392(10155),
1341-1348. https://doi.org/10.1016/S0140-6736(18)31928-7

Texas Health and Human Services. (2023). WIC Breastfeeding.
https://www.hhs.texas.gov/providers/wic-providers/
wic-breastfeeding#:~:text=Lactation%20Hotline%3A%20
855%2D550%2D,available%20to%20anyone%20in%20
Texas.

The Breastfeeding Center of Ann Arbor. (2023). Cost of Formula
Feeding. https://bfcaa.com/resources/cost-of-formula-
feeding/#:~:text=If%20you%20buy%20a%20name,11%20
per%20oz.

About the author:

Elizabeth De Luna is a stay-at-home mom of three children. She left her job as a librarian to spend more time with her family and homeschool her children. She often gives advice to new parents around her, so she decided to write a book to help new parents everywhere. You can find her on Instagram at @enlightenedelizabeth, or you can email her questions at elizabethgracedeluna@gmail.com.